First World War
and Army of Occupation
War Diary
France, Belgium and Germany

40 DIVISION
119 Infantry Brigade
Duke of Cambridge's Own (Middlesex Regiment)
21st Battalion
1 February 1918 - 30 June 1918

WO95/2606/3

The Naval & Military Press Ltd
www.nmarchive.com
Published in association with The National Archives

Published by

The Naval & Military Press Ltd

Unit 10 Ridgewood Industrial Park,

Uckfield, East Sussex,

TN22 5QE England

Tel: +44 (0) 1825 749494

www.naval-military-press.com

www.nmarchive.com

This diary has been reprinted in facsimile from the original. Any imperfections are inevitably reproduced and the quality may fall short of modern type and cartographic standards.

© Crown Copyright
Images reproduced by permission of The National Archives, London, England, 2015.

Contents

Document type	Place/Title	Date From	Date To
War Diary	WO95/2606/3 21 Battalion Middlesex Regiment		
Heading	40th Division 119th Infy Bde 21st Bn Middx Regt Feb-Jun 1918 From 121 Bde 40 Div To-UK		
Heading	40th Division. 119th Infantry Brigade. War Diary 21st Battalion The Middlesex Regiment March 1918		
Heading	21st (S) Bn. Middlesex Regt. March 1st-31st Vol 22		
War Diary	Gouy-En-Artois	01/03/1918	03/03/1918
War Diary	Hendecourt Les-Ransart	04/03/1918	12/03/1918
War Diary	Mercatel Area	13/03/1918	26/03/1918
War Diary	Bucquoy	26/03/1918	26/03/1918
War Diary	Bienvillers	27/03/1918	27/03/1918
War Diary	Sombrin	28/03/1918	29/03/1918
War Diary	La Comte	30/03/1918	31/03/1918
Miscellaneous	Narrative Of events during Operation in the Neighbourhood of Croisilles, St. Leger, Mory, and Ervillers, From the 91st to 26th March 1918 Appendix I	26/03/1918	26/03/1918
Miscellaneous	Narrative of events during operations in the Neighbourhood of Croisilles, St. Leger, Mory, and Ervillers, from the 91st to 26th March 1918. Appendix I	01/04/1918	01/04/1918
Heading	40th Division. 119th Infantry Brigade. War Diary 21st Battalion The Middlesex Regiment April 1918		
Heading	War Diary 21st (S) Bn. Middx Regt. April 1918 Vol 23		
War Diary	La Comte	01/04/1918	01/04/1918
War Diary	Sailly-Sur-La-Lys.	02/04/1918	03/04/1918
War Diary	Fleurbaix Sector	04/04/1918	09/04/1918
War Diary	Steenwerck Switch	10/04/1918	10/04/1918
War Diary	Le Verrier	11/04/1918	11/04/1918
War Diary	Strazeele	12/04/1918	13/04/1918
War Diary	Staple	13/04/1918	13/04/1918
War Diary	Tilques	14/04/1918	17/04/1918
War Diary	Moulle	18/04/1918	20/04/1918
War Diary	Petit Difques	21/04/1918	29/04/1918
War Diary	Seninghem	30/04/1918	30/04/1918
Miscellaneous	Narrative Of Operations Of 21st (S) Bn Middlesex Regt From 9th To 13th April 1918	16/04/1918	16/04/1918
Heading	21st Middlesex Regt Feby 1st-28th 1918 Vol 21		
War Diary	Left Sub-Sector Centre Brigade Bullecourt	01/02/1918	05/02/1918
War Diary	Support Battalion Left Brigade	05/02/1918	08/02/1918
War Diary	Left Sub-Sector Left Brigade	09/02/1918	11/02/1918
War Diary	Mory	12/02/1918	12/02/1918
War Diary	Mercatel	13/02/1918	22/02/1918
War Diary	Hendecourt (Blaireville Area)	23/02/1918	28/02/1918
Heading	War Diary Of 21st (S) Bn. Middlesex Regiment for May 1918 Vol 24		
War Diary	Seninghem	01/05/1918	03/05/1918
War Diary	Bonneghem	04/05/1918	09/05/1918
War Diary	P.20.C. 4.5.	10/05/1918	18/05/1918
War Diary	O. 24.b. 5.0.	19/05/1918	31/05/1918
Heading	21st (S) Bn. Middlesex Regt. War Diary June 1918 Vol 25		

War Diary	St. Marie Capelle	01/06/1918	02/06/1918
War Diary	Wacquinghen	03/06/1918	10/06/1918
War Diary	Hardinghen	11/06/1918	11/06/1918
War Diary	Haut Loquin	12/06/1918	16/06/1918
War Diary	Alquines	17/06/1918	28/06/1918
War Diary	Boulogne	29/06/1918	29/06/1918
War Diary	Mytchett Aldershot	30/06/1918	30/06/1918

WO95/2606/3
21 Battalion Middlesex Regiment

40TH DIVISION
119TH INFY BDE

21ST BN MIDDX REGT
FEB - JUN 1918

From 121 Bde 40 Div
To UK

40th Division.
119th Infantry Brigade.

WAR DIARY

21st BATTALION

THE MIDDLESEX REGIMENT

MARCH 1918

Attached :- Narrative of Operations 21st-26th

Army Form C. 2118.

WAR DIARY
or
INTELLIGENCE SUMMARY.
(Erase heading not required.)

CONFIDENTIAL
21ST (S) BN. MIDDLESEX REGT.
March 1st – 31st

SHEETS. I – IV.

H. Metcalfe Lieut-Col.
Comdg 21st (S) Bn Middlesex Regt.

Army Form C. 2118.

WAR DIARY
or
INTELLIGENCE SUMMARY.
(Erase heading not required.) CONFIDENTIAL

Sheet T.

Instructions regarding War Diaries and Intelligence Summaries are contained in F. S. Regs., Part II. and the Staff Manual respectively. Title pages will be prepared in manuscript.

Place	Date	Hour	Summary of Events and Information	Remarks and references to Appendices
GOUY-EN-ARTOIS	March 1918	Ref 51.c S.E. 1/20,000		
	1		Test alarm message received at 8.15 am and Battn moved off at 9.20 am. Order received en route at MONCHIET to proceed on route march. Battn arrived back in billets at 2.30 pm.	(1)
	2		Training carried out during morning from 8.30 am to 12.30 pm, football in afternoon.	(11)
			A.F. B213 d/28/2/18 Effective strength 51 Offs 1006 O.R.	(3)
	3		Battalion forwarded by march route to BLAREVILLE AREA leaving billets at 10.20 am and arriving at No 5 Camp HENDECOURT-LES-RANSART at 2 pm. No further parades	(4)
HENDECOURT LES-RANSART	4		Lt. Col. Le Mottelé resumed command of the Battn on returning from short leave. Company training including musketry PT+BF bombing close order drill carried out from 8.30 am to 12.30 pm and specialist training in afternoon.	(4)
	5		Battn carried out trench to trench attack scheme during morning, specialist training in afternoon.	(5)
	6		Battn carried out Brigade route attack scheme hill 1 pm. No further parade. Recreation training in afternoon.	(5)
	7		Same operation carried out today as yesterday. Recreational training in afternoon.	(6)

WAR DIARY or INTELLIGENCE SUMMARY

Army Form C. 2118.

Sheet II

(Erase heading not required.) CONFIDENTIAL.

Place	Date 1918	Hour	Summary of Events and Information	Remarks and references to Appendices
HENDECOURT LES-RANSART	8		Ref 51 SE 1/20000 : 51 SW 1/20000. Inspection by G.O.C. VI Corps. Special training from 1.30pm to 3.30pm.	
	9		Battalion on the Attack scheme during morning. Recreational training in afternoon.	
			At 1315 dates 9/3/18 effective strength 55 officers 1049 O.R.	
	10		Battalion attended Divisional Church Service. No other parades.	
	11		Special training from 8.30am to 11.30am. Battalion practice the attack in co-operation with Tanks from 1.30pm to 4pm	
	12		Company and Platoon training from 8.30am to 12.30pm. In accordance with orders (?Battn: manual) constituting the Reorganised Establishment as laid down in SS 135, moved to the MERCATEL AREA at 6pm. Arrived at DURHAM CAMP at 1.30pm. Remainder of Battn remain at Brigade Details Camp in BLAIREVILLE AREA. Whilst in this area Battn to parade between 8.30am and 12km	
MERCATEL AREA	13		Company training including close order drill, P.T & B.F, bombing, musketry and rapid practice during the whole hours.	
	14		Usual training from 8 to 8 to 12.30pm & 1.30pm to 5pm	
	15		Feet alone inspection paraded at 6.30 am. Battalion paraded at 9 am &	

Army Form C. 2118.

Sheet III

WAR DIARY
or
INTELLIGENCE SUMMARY.

CONFIDENTIAL

(Erase heading not required.)

Instructions regarding War Diaries and Intelligence Summaries are contained in F.S. Regs., Part II. and the Staff Manual respectively. Title pages will be prepared in manuscript.

Place	Date 1918	Hour	Summary of Events and Information	Remarks and references to Appendices
MERCATEL AREA	15		Ref 51b SW 1/20,000. At 1 pm Brigade informed that returns received to stand-down and assume normal condition. Company relief training from 9.30 am.	
	16		Maneuvers. Draining during work hours in morning. Recreational training in afternoon. AF B213 dated 16/3/18 Effective Strength 54 Off 976 OR	
	17		Training carried out from 7am to 8am & 9am to 6.1pm. Working party of 350 OR for Burying cable at 6 pm. Battalion furnished working party. 1.45 am 18/3/18	
	18		Ceremonial drill between 12 non. & 1 pm. Working party of 500 OR furnished at same time and for same purpose as yesterday; returned to Camp 1.15 am 19/3/18	
	19		Ceremonial drill between 12 & 1 pm. Same working party found as for yesterday; returned to Camp 12.15 am 20/3/18.	
	20		No parades to-day. Same working party found.	
	21 22 23 24 25 26		For resumé of operations during this period see Appendix 1 attached AF B213 dated 23/3/18 Effective Strength 54 Off 960 OR.	

Army Form C. 2118.

Sheet IV.

WAR DIARY
or
INTELLIGENCE SUMMARY.
(Erase heading not required.)

CONFIDENTIAL

Instructions regarding War Diaries and Intelligence Summaries are contained in F. S. Regs., Part II. and the Staff Manual respectively. Title pages will be prepared in manuscript.

Place	Date March 1918	Hour	Summary of Events and Information	Remarks and references to Appendices
BUCQUOY	26	5am	of LENS 11 1/100.000. Battalion arrived here after being withdrawn from the line. Marched off again at 7.30 am and arrived at BIENVILLERS at 1 pm. At 2.30 pm a message was received that the enemy had broken through HEBUTERNE and Battn was ordered to occupy the ridge S of BUCQUOY. This position was occupied for remainder of the day.	
BIENVILLERS	27	2.15pm	Battn ordered to withdraw and proceed to WANQUETIN Area, Battn was afterwards ordered to SOMBRIN. After a march of 15 miles the Battn arrived in billets at SOMBRIN at about 11 am, no men falling out en route.	
SOMBRIN	28		All details left behind on 21st inst rejoined Battn from GAUDIEMPRÉ during recent operations — Killed 2 Off + 21 OR.; Total casualties sustained wounded — 6 Off + 18A OR., 3 Wounded missing 6 OR.; Missing 1 Off + 80 OR.	
	29.		Battn left by motor route for LA COMTÉ at 8 am. Part of Battn engaged in recent operations were to proceed by lorries to TINCQUES but a majority of men had to proceed on foot. Arriving in billets at 7 pm	
LA COMTÉ	30		Day spent in cleaning up and checking stores. A.F. B213 d/30/3/18 Effective Strength 45 Off 665 OR.	
	31		Church parade during morning, no further parades.	

H.C. Metcalf Lt-Col
Cmdg 2nd Bn Middlesex Regt.

Ref. Map. 51. B. 57. C.

Appendix 1.

Narrative of events during operations in the neighbourhood of CROISILLES, ST. LEGER, MORY, and ERVILLERS, from the 21st to 26th March, 1918.

21st March. On the morning of the 21st March when the enemy commenced his offensive, the Battalion was stationed at DURHAM "A" LINES, BOISLEUX-AU-MONT.

Between 5 & 6 p.m., the Battalion was ordered to proceed forthwith to position of assembly "F" North of BOIRY BECQUERELLE, and to seize HENIN HILL and to deny it to the enemy. This was accomplished without opposition, the second line system on the HILL being found to be occupied by troops of the 3rd and 34th Divisions. The troops from these Divisions were also in trenches in advance of this system. The Battalion therefore took up its position in depth on a frontage of about 1400 yards front, and pushed out reconnoitring Patrols to endeavour to gain touch with the enemy.

22nd. March. In accordance with orders received, the Battalion was
3 a.m. withdrawn, and marched to position in SENSEE VALLEY, North of ERVILLERS, B.8.a., in reserve to the Brigade which was holding the third system near ST. LEGER. A position was taken up in the ARMY LINE, which ran across SENSEE VALLEY. The Battalion was in touch with the 13th East Surreys on the right, and troops of the Royal Engineers on the left, on the BAPAUME-ARRAS ROAD.

2 p.m. 22nd March. "D" Company was ordered up to reinforce the 18th Battalion Welsh Regiment in CROISILLES SWITCH in neighbourhood of JUDAS FARM.

6 p.m. 22nd March. "D" Company reported that British troops in front of them were withdrawing, and "D" Company were engaged with the adv[ancing enemy] in conjunction with the 18th Welsh. The [enemy were] reported to be occupying ST. LEGER.

D Company. There is no mention of this company in diary of 18 Welsh Regt.

Ref. Map. 51. B. 57. C.

Appendix 1.

Narrative of events during operations in the neighbourhood of CROISILLES, ST. LEGER, MORY, and ERVILLERS, from the 21st to 26th March, 1918.

21st March. On the morning of the 21st March when the enemy commenced his offensive, the Battalion was stationed at DURHAM "A" LINES, BOISLEUX-AU-MONT.

Between 5 & 6 p.m., the Battalion was ordered to proceed forthwith to position of assembly "F" North of BOIRY BECQUERELLE, and to seize HENIN HILL and to deny it to the enemy. This was accomplished without opposition, the second line system on the HILL being found to be occupied by troops of the 3rd and 34th Divisions. The troops from these Divisions were also in trenches in advance of this system. The Battalion therefore took up its position in depth on a frontage of about 1400 yards front, and pushed out reconnoitring patrols to endeavour to gain touch with the enemy.

22nd March. In accordance with orders received, the Battalion was
3 a.m. withdrawn, and marched to position in SENSEE VALLEY, North of ERVILLERS, B.8.a., in reserve to the Brigade which was holding the third system near ST. LEGER. A position was taken up in the ARMY LINE, which ran across SENSEE VALLEY. The Battalion was in touch with the 13th East Surreys on the right, and troops of the Royal Engineers on the left, on the BAPAUME-ARRAS ROAD.

2 p.m. 22nd March. "D" Company was ordered up to reinforce the 18th Battalion Welsh Regiment in CROISILLES SWITCH in neighbourhood of JUDAS FARM.

6 p.m. 22nd March. "D" Company reported that British troops in front of them were withdrawing, and shortly afterwards "D" Company were engaged with the advancing enemy in conjunction with the 18th Welsh. The enemy were then reported to be occupying ST. LEGER.

(2)

6-30 a.m. 23rd March.	The Brigade Major visited Battalion Headquarters, and gave verbal orders to concentrate at once, and to launch an attack on Mory in conjunction with the 13th East Surreys, who were to operate on the right, and with the 18th Welsh in reserve, to regain the Village and the Army Line running North-east and East of the Village. The Battalion at the time was widely extended in the Army Line across the SENSEE VALLEY, and "D" Company was still in CROISILLES SWITCH.
8 a.m.	The Battalion was concentrated in quarries etc., B.Q.c., and orders were issued to Company Commanders with regard to the attack. As by now it was considered that sufficient time had elapsed to allow the East Surreys to get into position on the right, and as they were actually seen deploying South of
8-45 a.m.	ERVILLERS, zero hour was fixed as 8-45, and the attack commenced. The attack was launched on a two Company front, with the left flank directing, and advancing along the Army Line. One Company was in support with two platoons in echelon from the right of the right Company, whose orders were to obtain touch with the East Surreys as soon as possible. One Company remained in Battalion reserve. At zero "A" & "B" Companies formed up on the ST. LEGER-ERVILLERS ROAD, and moved off in artillery formation, preceded by scouts. On arriving at the ridge, B.15.a., a considerable amount of machine gun fire was encountered, and the leading troops deployed, the advance continuing without a break. There was not much hostile shelling at the time.
9 a.m.	Our artillery opened, but it very much under-estimated the range, and the majority of the shells fell amongst, or burst amongst over our men, causing several casualties. This was communicated to Brigade Headquarters and the Artillery, and the range ultimately lengthened. Notwithstanding continuous machine gun fire,

21 M'sex

the advance continued very steadily in short rushes, one section or Lewis Gun team covering the advance of another. On approaching the Army Line, it was found that the enemy were not actually holding it, but had taken up a position on the further side of the wire, whence they enfiladed our advancing troops.

10-30 a.m. In view of the extended nature of our line, and the fact that a report was received that the body of the enemy were advancing from the direction of MORY COPSE, the reserve Company was thrown in, and a request for further reinforcements sent to the Brigade. This resulted in a Company of the 18th Welsh being placed at our disposal, and this Company was ordered to dig itself in 400 yards in rear of our right flank for the purpose of counter attack, if this should be necessary. This Company eventually resolved itself into a refused flank at right angles to the Army Line facing MORY.

11-15 a.m. Officer Commanding "C" Company, who arrived at the Aid Post wounded, reported that his men were very close to MORY, and on the Railway Embankment North-East. As this party has not been seen since, it is presumed that they were cut off. As the advance continued, the Army Line was manned by parties attached from the left flank, until it was fully garrisoned as far as B.15.d.9.9. An enemy strong point in MORY COPSE and machine guns in MORY gave the men a hot reception, and by the time the Army Line had been reached, the strength had been too much reduced by casualties to admit of further progress in the direction of MORY. Also about this time a message was received from the Brigade Major saying that one Company of the East Surreys would assist our advance by attacking MORY from ERVILLERS in a E.S.E. direction. It was then realized that the amount of co-operation which the East Surreys were apparently able to afford would make it impracticable for this Battalion to press home the attack on MORY, and at the same time comply with the instructions to keep touch with the Guards in the Army Line on our left. This latter objective having been reached, the action was broken off, and orders issued to consolidate in depth, and if possible to send Patrols into MORY.

During the course of the advance a hostile aeroplane flew low along our line, firing its machine gun at our troops, and hindering the advance. This plane was successfully brought down by a Lewis Gunner. It crashed N.E. of MORY behind the enemy lines.

The Army Line was found to be dug to the depth of 1 ft. 6 in. only, and very broad. This afforded very little cover to our men, who were enfiladed on both flanks from MORY on the right, and from a communication trench on the left. Movement about the Army Line was further hindered by the fact that 300 yards of it had not even been dug. This block occurred almost in the middle of our new line, and the ground was under full observation by the enemy, and swept by machine gun fire. Communication, however, was maintained at intervals by runners, who worked exceedingly well, and at dusk a telephone line was run out. Throughout the day the movements of the enemy south of ST. LEGER were clearly visible, and on several occasions information was sent back to the Artillery of the massing of troops, transport, etc., and on every occasion great disorder and many casualties were caused by their fire. The Lewis Gunners had an unlimited number of targets, but the necessity of keeping a reserve of ammunition for any attack prevented the gunners from taking full advantage of them.

The troops carried out the attack in the best possible order, and with magnificent dash, more as though they were on a field day than in a battle.

At dusk the consolidation of the line was continued, and what troops were available commenced to dig a trench through the undug portion. By the time it was handed over to the relieving Battalion on the 24th, only 50 yards remained undug.

The night of the 23rd/24th passed quietly. During the night the 118th Trench Mortar Battery brought up a Stokes Gun to retaliate on the enemy machine gun in the communication trench about B.V.a.1.3., and it was found the following day that the enemy had also brought up a trench mortar battery, which enfiladed our line and caused several casualties. The Artillery eventually dealt with this battery.

24th March.
Several times during the day our Artillery fired on MORY COPSE, and enemy movements behind their lines. A daylight patrol under Sgt. Hickman brought in a prisoner from near MORY COPSE.

10-30 p.m.
The enemy broke through at the spot where the trench had been left undug. They came through in massed formation and spread on either flank, surrounding several bodies of our men. The signaller on duty in the front trench saw the enemy when he reached our wire, and immediately rang up Headquarters and sent the S.O.S. signal until it was answered. Being by this time surrounded, he smashed his Fullerphone and joined in the fighting. The Artillery barrage was put down with extraordinary rapidity, but unfortunately in many places it was again short, and caused further disorganization. It however caused very heavy casualties to the assailants. Taken in the rear, parties of men had to give way, but for the most part rejoined their Companies. An attempt was made subsequently to restore the

Army Line, but as the right flank was now right in the air, the remainder of the Battalion commenced to dig a new line at right angles to the Army Line, and parallel with the ST. LEGER-ERVILLERS ROAD, touch being maintained with troops on both flanks.

Hot food, rations and ammunition were hurried up. During the course of this attack at least 50 prisoners were taken by the Battalion, and sent back. For the most part these were used to carry our wounded from the Aid Post.

25th March. Soon after dawn it was evident that the enemy intended to attack ERVILLERS, as parties of them were observed in every direction on the ridges. No definite action, however, was taken by the enemy, and several barrages were put down by our Artillery during the day. Air craft also were very active, two of our planes being brought down near ERVILLERS.

3 p.m. About the middle of the afternoon information was received from Brigade Headquarters that the enemy had occupied BEHAGNIES, and were advancing on ERVILLERS. To prevent an enveloping movement from GOMIECOURT on the part of the enemy, the Battalion was ordered to take up a position WEST of ERVILLERS. this movement was effected under heavy artillery fire. From this point a rearguard action was carried out until, in accordance with

6.30 p.m. instructions, a trench system was occupied south of HAMELINCOURT, touch being maintained on the right with the East Surreys and the East Yorks, and troops of the 42nd Division.

26th March.
3 a.m. During the course of the night instructions were received to retire via Courcelles to HUCQUOY, and this was carried out without incident.

1.4.18

H.C. Metcalfe Lt. Col.
Comdg 21/Middlesex Regt

40th Division.
119th Infantry Brigade.

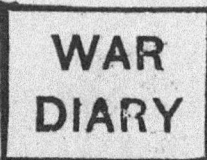

21st BATTALION

THE MIDDLESEX REGIMENT

APRIL 1 9 1 8

Appendix attached:- Report on Operations
9th - 13th April

Army Form C. 2118.

WAR DIARY
or
INTELLIGENCE SUMMARY.
(Erase heading not required.)

WAR DIARY
21st (s) Bn. MIDDX. REGT.
for
APRIL - 1918

Army Form C. 2118.

WAR DIARY
or
INTELLIGENCE SUMMARY.
(Erase heading not required.)

APRIL 1918.

Instructions regarding War Diaries and Intelligence Summaries are contained in F. S. Regs., Part II. and the Staff Manual respectively. Title pages will be prepared in manuscript.

Place	Date	Hour	Summary of Events and Information	Remarks and references to Appendices
LA COMTE	1/4/18		Bright fine morning - visibility good. The Battalion moved from LA COMTE in the early morning to DOULIEU, first by march route to BERLIN, and thence by light railway. Engine running off the line delayed the journey by 3 hours.	
SAILLY-SUR-LA-LYS.	2/4/18		Day fine. The Battalion moved from DOULIEU to SAILLY-SUR-LA-LYS, and came into Brigade Reserve.	
	3/4/18		Wet morning. The Battalion was ordered into support to the 120th Infantry Brigade which was holding the RIGHT SUB-SECTOR of the FLEURBAIX SYSTEM. Battalion moved up, but returned to billets upon receiving cancellation of order, and came under orders to man a portion of the system of trenches on the RIGHT flank of the Brigade facing S.W. towards LAVENTIE in the event of the Brigade on the RIGHT (PORTUGUESE) giving way.	
FLEURBAIX SECTOR	4/4/18		Damp and raining at times. The O.C. reconnoitred in the morning the defences that the Battalion would have to take up while the Brigade was in Reserve. In the afternoon the Battalion came under the orders of the G.O.C. 120th Brigade, and moved into support on the RIGHT SUB-SECTOR	
	5/4/18		Dull. The C.O. reconnoitred the reserve lines of the Brigade in the RIGHT SUB-SECTOR, and trained company commanders.	

Army Form C. 2118.

WAR DIARY
INTELLIGENCE SUMMARY.
(Erase heading not required.)

APRIL 1918

Instructions regarding War Diaries and Intelligence Summaries are contained in F. S. Regs., Part II. and the Staff Manual respectively. Title pages will be prepared in manuscript.

Place	Date	Hour	Summary of Events and Information	Remarks and references to Appendices
	6/4/18		Fine and warm. During the day intermittent shelling of billets. C.O. inspected the Companies. At 8 p.m. the Battalion came under the orders of 119th Brigade, which relieved the 120th Brigade in the line.	
	7/4/18		Dull, with bright intervals. All available men in the Battalion were bathed during the morning. The G.O.C. 119th Infantry Brigade visited B.H.Q.	
	8/4/18		Misty. Battalion Headquarters was heavily shelled in the morning. C.O. visited Company Commanders. Alterations were made in the disposition of Lewis Guns in the Defence Scheme.	
	9/4/18	4.15 a.m	Misty and damp. 4.15 a.m. enemy started heavy bombardment of all billets. The Battalion "Stood to" and on receiving S.O.S. from RIGHT. Battalion moved up into Battle positions. Capt. G.F.P. Worthington was sent to report to Brigade Headquarters in accordance with the Defence Scheme. Heavy Casualties were inflicted owing to the enemy shelling.	
		9.30 am	At about 9.30 a.m. a message was received that the enemy had penetrated our front system of trenches.	
		10.15 am	At about 10.15 a.m. 2 Companies of the Battalion were ordered up to reinforce Machine Gun Line. At the same hour it was found that the enemy had broken through on the PORTUGUESE FRONT and were advancing on Battalion Headquarters.	
		11 am	At about 11 am the Second-in-Command was killed, and the Adjutant wounded: Battalion Headquarters had already been moved back into a trench close by.	

Army Form C. 2118.

WAR DIARY
— of —
INTELLIGENCE SUMMARY.
(Erase heading not required.)

Instructions regarding War Diaries and Intelligence Summaries are contained in F. S. Regs., Part II. and the Staff Manual respectively. Title pages will be prepared in manuscript.

APRIL 1918

Place	Date	Hour	Summary of Events and Information	Remarks and references to Appendices
			Owing to enemy pressure Battalion Headquarters was again moved back to SAILLY STN. Eventually, with reinforcements, a line was taken up in front of RUE DU QUESNOY.	
		4 p.m.	At 4 p.m. enemy having entered SAILLY, remnants of Battalion were withdrawn across RIVER LYS and occupied STEENWERCK SWITCH.	
		4.30 p.m.	At 4.30 p.m. the Quartermaster blew up the Stores at SAILLY and crossed the RIVER. Enemy were encountered on LEFT Bank of RIVER.	
STEENWERCK SWITCH	10/4/18		STEENWERCK SWITCH was heavily shelled in the early morning, and later enfiladed with Machine Gun fire. Later in the day to conform with line on the RIGHT, the Battalion, with men from remnants of other units, withdrew, and dug-in in front of LE PETIT MORTIER.	
LE VERRIER	11/4/18		The enemy pressure was very great at about 8 a.m. At this stage the C.O. Lt. Col. H.C. METCALFE was wounded, and CAPT. G.F.P. WORTHINGTON took over Command of the remnants of the Battalion. Throughout the day the Battalion withdrew by stages, and eventually took up a position in front of LE VERRIER in conformity with the rest of the line.	
STRAZEELE	12/4/18		During the early morning, in accordance with orders received from Brigade H.Q. the Battalion withdrew from the line to STRAZEELE, having been replaced by Battalions of the 31st Division.	
		2 p.m.	After feeding and resting, the Battalion was ordered to dig a defensive position S.E. of STRAZEELE in touch with the 13th East Surreys on the LEFT and the 121st Infantry Brigade on the RIGHT.	

Army Form C. 2118

WAR DIARY
or
INTELLIGENCE SUMMARY.
(Erase heading not required.)

APRIL 1918

Instructions regarding War Diaries and Intelligence Summaries are contained in F. S. Regs., Part II. and the Staff Manual respectively. Title pages will be prepared in manuscript.

Place	Date	Hour	Summary of Events and Information	Remarks references to Appendices
	13/4/18		Fine morning. During the morning the new defences were heavily shelled by the enemy.	
STAPLE		1 pm	At 1 pm orders were received to withdraw the Battalion to N. of PRADELLES. From where the Battalion marched to HONDEGHEM where a hot meal was given to the men.	
		6 pm	At 6 pm the Battalion marched to CROSS ROADS 1 mile E. of STAPLE, where it was billeted for the night.	
TILQUES.	14/4/18		In the early morning the Brigade marched from STAPLE to TILQUES. A 2 hours halt was ordered in the middle of the day at ARQUES for feeding and resting the men.	
	15/4/18		The O.C. visited the men in their billets where they were resting out.	
	16/4/18		In the morning the Battalion carried Physical drill and inspections of men were carried out, and in the afternoon the men rested.	
	17/4/18		The Battalion carried out training on an area allotted to it in the neighbourhood of TILQUES. Special attention being given in Musketry by Instructors from the Army School of Musketry.	
MOULLE	18/4/18		The Battalion moved into billets at MOULLE leaving 1 Company behind to be absorbed into the 121st Composite Brigade.	
	19/4/18		Orders were received to hold in readiness 2 Officers and 200 men to proceed to 12th Bn. Middlesex Regt.	

Army Form C. 2118.

WAR DIARY
or
INTELLIGENCE SUMMARY.
(Erase heading not required.)

APRIL 1918.

Instructions regarding War Diaries and Intelligence Summaries are contained in F. S. Regs., Part II. and the Staff Manual respectively. Title pages will be prepared in manuscript.

Place	Date	Hour	Summary of Events and Information	Remarks and references to Appendices
MOULLE	20/4/18		A further 1 Officer and 98 O.R. were sent to the 121st Composite Brigade.	
PETIT DIFQUES	21/4/18		The reinforcements for the 1st Bn were despatched, and the Battalion under the orders of the Brigade moved from MOULLE by march route into billets at PETIT DIFQUES.	
	22/4/18		The C.O. inspected the men in their billets. Close order drill and Physical Training was carried out.	
	23/4/18		Close order drill and physical training carried out.	
	24/4/18		Instruction in Musketry, Close order drill, and physical training carried out. Weather misty.	
	25/4/18		Instruction in Musketry, close order drill, and physical training carried out.	
	26/4/18		Physical training and close order drill carried out.	
	27/4/18		Physical training and close order drill carried out.	
	28/4/18		Church Parade in the morning.	
	29/4/18		Physical exercise in the morning followed by baths.	

Army Form C. 2118.

WAR DIARY
INTELLIGENCE SUMMARY.
(Erase heading not required.)

APRIL 1918.

Place	Date	Hour	Summary of Events and Information	Remarks and references to Appendices
SENINGHEM	30/4/18		The Battalion moved from PETIT DIFQUES by march route into billets at SENINGHEM	

NARRATIVE OF OPERATIONS OF
21ST (s) BN. MIDDLESEX REGT
FROM 9TH TO 13TH APRIL 1918

9th April.- On the morning of the 9th the Battalion was in Brigade Support in sector between LAVENTIE and FLEURBAIX. At 4am enemy commenced a heavy bombardment of billets, all Headquarters, being particularly heavily shelled, thereby showing enemy's knowledge of their positions. A lot of gas shells mixed with H.E. were sent over. At 4-10am the Battalion stood to in the vicinity of billets, and on receiving S.O.S. from right, Battalion moved up into battle positions. The bombardment then showed no signs of diminishing. At 10am "C" & "D" Companies were ordered up to occupy Machine Gun Line. This was not occupied, owing to having been seized by the enemy. These two Companies then occupied a line South East of the Rue du Queones in about H.27.c. At 10.15am the enemy was found to be in the neighbourhood of ROUGE DE BOUT, and

(2)

was advancing in a north-easterly direction towards SAILLY, BAC ST MAUR and FLEURBAIX. Owing to enemy encircling movements Battalion H.Qs were withdrawn in short stages to strong point in front of SAILLY, having then lost more than half of personnel in casualties, including the Adjutant and Second in command. At about this time the

details ~~Battalion~~ from SAILLY, which had been ordered up by Brigade, arrived and encountered enemy on Road from ROUGE DE BOUT to SAILLY at about G.36.a. A line was taken up by the ~~Battalion~~ in front of RUE DU QUESNOY at about G.29.d. At about 4 pm, owing to the enemy having entered SAILLY, the remnants of the Battalion were withdrawn across river LYS by bridge in G.16.b, moving then to occupy the STEENWERCK SWITCH. This bridge was then blown up by the R.E.

At 4.30 pm the Quartermaster, being unable to remove stores from SAILLY, set fire to them, and withdrew over River with details from Q.Ms Stores, posting C.Q.Ms SKELLY and GILES with Lewis guns on north-east side of River LYS to

(3)

defend River bridge.

    Early in the evening enemy was found to have crossed River LYS in neighbourhood of BAC ST MAUR, and the rest of the evening and night passed without incident of importance.

10th April. – At 3.45 am the enemy heavily shelled STEENWERCK SWITCH in enfilade. About midday the SWITCH was enfiladed with machine gun fire. The troops on the right having withdrawn, the Battalion fell back to conform with line on right, and dug in front of PETIT MORTIER. The Battalion was then much intermixed with 12th Yorks and units of 25th Division, the right flank being in touch with the 120th and the left with the 121st Brigade. The remainder of the day and night passed without incident, except for interchange of rifle and machine gun fire.

11th April. – Towards 7 & 8 am the whole line withdrew by stages and took up a position in front of LE VERRIER. During this withdrawal the Commanding Officer became a casualty.

(4)

The rest of the day and night was quiet.

12th April.— In the early morning the Battalions of the 119th Brigade were ordered to withdraw to STRAZEELE, having been replaced by 31st Division. The Battalion was collected together at STRAZEELE and at about 4 p.m. was ordered to dig and occupy a defensive position to the South and Southeast of STRAZEEL. The left flank was in touch with the 13th Surreys, and the right flank with Cyclists, Australians and 121st Brigade.

13th April.— At about 2 p.m. orders were received for the Brigade to concentrate at ~~BAILLEUX~~ PRADELLES.

C.F.W. Worthington
Capt
16.4.18. Commanding 21st Bn. Middlesex Regt.

Army Form C. 2118.

WAR DIARY
or
INTELLIGENCE SUMMARY.
(Erase heading not required.)

CONFIDENTIAL

21st Middlesex Regt.

Feby. 1st – 28th 1918.

Place	Date	Hour	Summary of Events and Information	Remarks and references to Appendices

Army Form C. 2118.

Sheet 1

WAR DIARY
or
INTELLIGENCE SUMMARY.
(Erase heading not required.)

CONFIDENTIAL

Instructions regarding War Diaries and Intelligence Summaries are contained in F. S. Regs., Part II. and the Staff Manual respectively. Title pages will be prepared in manuscript.

Place	Date	Hour	Summary of Events and Information	Remarks and references to Appendices
LEFT SUB-SECTOR CENTRE BRIGADE BULLECOURT	1918 Feb		Ref. BULLECOURT 51⁰ SW 4 1/10,000	
	1		Battn relieved 20th Bn Middlesex Regt in Left Sub-Sector, relief complete 10.30 pm. Weather frosty. No unusual occurrence. Casualties nil	AP
	2		Disposition of Battn — A in right front line. D in left front line. C in support. B in reserve. Intermittent hostile shelling of the front line during morning. Ref B 21 B daOa 2/2/18. Effective strength 42 Off. 661 OR. Casualties nil	AP
	3		Nothing of interest happened today. Enemy quiet. Inter-Company relief took place. B & C Coy relieving A & D Coy respectively. Casualties nil	AP AP
	4		Enemy very quiet, nothing unusual to report. Casualties nil	AP
	5		Battn relieved by 20th Manch Regt. War completion of relief Battn returned to "Left Brigade" 17th Bdes Regt in support. O.C. 119th Brigade.	AP
SUPPORT BATTALION LEFT BRIGADE			Disposition — BHQ in Railway Reserve Excavations U25B. A Coy in MAN SUPPORT B & C in Railway Reserve, D Coy in MAIDA VALE. Enemy artillery very active during early morning of 5th. Casualties nil.	
	6		Battn in support. Working parties found for both front line Battalion. Went R.O. duty formed to Abbreviations Common. Casualties nil.	AP
	7		Working parties found as for previous day. Half Battn billetted at ST LEGER	AP

WAR DIARY or INTELLIGENCE SUMMARY.

Army Form C. 2118.

Sheet II

Place	Date	Hour	Summary of Events and Information	Remarks and references to Appendices
	1917		CONFIDENTIAL 51.S.W.4 1/10,000	
SUPPORT BN. LEFT BRIGADE	8		Ref. BULLECOURT. Working parties from 9.30 am to 12.30 pm and 5.30 pm to 9.30 pm. Remainder of Bath. ration relieved 15th West. Regt in left sub-sector in support of Brigade. Relief completed at 6.20 pm. Disposition:- A Coy in Rgt Front line, D Coy in Left Front line, C Coy in support in BURG SUPPORT, B Coy in Reserve in STRAY RESERVE. Patrols out all night as no signs of enemy. Enemy artillery active. Casualties nil	[X]
LEFT SUB-SECTOR LEFT BRIGADE	9		Front patrolled by night, ramparts manned at [stand to] by day. Considerable amount of enemy movement in BULLECOURT seen. A quiet day with exception of short bombardment of our line at 5.30 pm. Work of clearing trenches proceeded with. Casualties - nil	[X]
	10		Hostile artillery very active today. Patrol ramparts out as usual. Support & Reserve Coys supply working parties for clearing trenches. Casualties:- 3 O.R. killed, 1 O.R. wounded. Effective strength of Off. 26 OR.	[X]
	11		Bath relieved by 1/6th Nor'hmbd Fus. in 59 Div. On completion of relief Bath marched to MORT L'ABBAYE Camp.	
	12		Bath left MORT at 10.30 am and marched to NORTHUMBERLAND CAMP, MERCATEL arriving at 2.30 pm. Capt R.L. Hornby, Capt J. Elliott, Capt J. Kilgour, L Pl [Sidgen], 11 Arm bet Ord Pte as [Dunsing] Lt A Cliffe, 2nd Lt [H] Jacobs	[X]

Army Form C. 2118.

Sheet III

WAR DIARY
or
INTELLIGENCE SUMMARY.
(Erase heading not required.) CONFIDENTIAL

Instructions regarding War Diaries and Intelligence Summaries are contained in F. S. Regs., Part II. and the Staff Manual respectively. Title pages will be prepared in manuscript.

Place	Date 1918	Hour	Summary of Events and Information	Remarks and references to Appendices
MORY	12	Ref 51 SW 1/20,000	At 9.A.heavy thr. RJ Murray thr O/S relieves the 4th Lincs thr Major & thr LtCol. Parker and 300 OR joined the Batt from 1st Bn Wiltshire Regt. and the O.R. Coy from 15th Bn Hastings Regt	1 2
MERCATEL	13		raining. Church on duty from 9am -12.30pm + 2-3. Recreational Training	
	14		from 10 - 4. Work on Bayonet Course and Rate for Instruction against enemy	
	15		Bombing raids, Potato Patch and general improvement of Camp carried on	
	16		as a 2/3 Wilts 16. Effective Strength 56 Off 1016 OR	
	17		Church Parade; no further parades	3
	18		training carried on during morning. Battler proceeded by Decauville at	4
		10am	to NANCOURT for work on Corps line — Buggy. Jumny look	
			lorries 16.30pm. Batt. arrived back in Camp at (du) 12/7/18.	
	19		No parade during morning - training from 2 to 5 co-recreational training from 3-4	5
	20		training work carried on as usual	
	21		Reconnaissance of Corps Line by CO and Coy Commanders Western Ref G	6
	22		of COO. Found as for 18th inst. Bn arrived Back in Camp at 11.20am. Batt. moved to BLAIREVILLE Area + occupied Camp 105 vacated by	7

Army Form C. 2118.

Sheet iv

WAR DIARY
INTELLIGENCE SUMMARY

(Erase heading not required.)

CONFIDENTIAL

Place	Date	Hour	Summary of Events and Information	Remarks and references to Appendices
MEROICOURT	22 (cont) 1918		Ref. FRANCE Sheet 51c S.E. 1/20,000. 4th A+S.H. arrived in rest Camp at 12.15pm	
HENDECOURT (BLAIREVILLE AREA)	23		Training carried on during morning. Football tourney in afternoon.	
	24		Coy B Coy dinstalls Effective Strength 56 OR/1605 OR. Church Parade. Inspection of Coys by Reconnaissance of Coys by Senior Officers.	
	25		Training from 8.30a - 12.30p + 1.30 - 3. Musty Drill & Musketry (Bayt fracted)	
	26		Continued training	
	27		27/4/18 (Brigade Football Competition. Battalion defeated 18th H+L.I by 2 pts—nil	
	28		Battalion moved to BOISEUX Staging Area to billets in Govt. Ent. partis. 40th Brigade in GHQ Reserve	

A.M. Bowrn Major
Commanding 21st Middlesex Regt.

Army Form C. 2118.

WAR DIARY
or
INTELLIGENCE SUMMARY.
(Erase heading not required.)

WAR DIARY

of

21st (S) Bn. Middlesex Regiment

for May 1918

Army Form C. 2118.

WAR DIARY
INTELLIGENCE SUMMARY.
(Erase heading not required.)

MAY 1918.

Place	Date	Hour	Summary of Events and Information	Remarks and references to Appendices
SENINGHEM	1/5/18		Inspection by C.O. Physical training and close order drill carried out.	
	2/5/18		Inspection of Transport Limbers by C.O. Physical training, close order drill and musketry carried out.	
	3/5/18		The Battalion bathed. Physical training carried out.	
BONNEGHEM	4/5/18		Weather fine. The Battalion moved by march route to billets at BONNEGHEM. A halt of 1 hour was made for mid-day meal. The Officers and men who has been attached to the Composite Brigade rejoined Battalion.	
	5/5/18		The surplus personnel consisting of 1 Officer and 38 other ranks were despatched to the Base. The G.O.C. visited Battalion during morning.	
	6/5/18		Training Staff inspected by C.O.	
	7/5/18		Battalion marched to Baths at ST. MOMELIN. Physical training carried out.	
	8/5/18		Physical training and close order drill carried out.	

Army Form C. 2118.

WAR DIARY
or
INTELLIGENCE SUMMARY.
(Erase heading not required.)

MAY 1918.

Instructions regarding War Diaries and Intelligence Summaries are contained in F. S. Regs., Part II. and the Staff Manual respectively. Title pages will be prepared in manuscript.

Place	Date	Hour	Summary of Events and Information	Remarks and references to Appendices
BONNEGHEM	9/5/18	11:30	Inspection of Training Staff by C.O.	NIL
		2:30 pm	Harness inspection by the C.O.	NIL
			Ribbands were presented to N° 15558 Sgt J.E. Pike, N° 10677 Cpl. H. Sheels and N° 41047 Pte E.J. Card. who had been awarded the Military Medal.	NIL
P.20.c.4.5	10/5/18		Battalion moves by march route to rear areas and went under canvas in a field near ST MARIE CAPPEL at P.20.c.4.5. en parton by 4 pm. 2nd Lt R.W. MARLOW was left at BONNEGHEM in charge of the Transport.	NIL
	11/5/18		Training was carried out during the morning. A Reconnaissance of the new WINNEZEELE LINE was carried out by C.O. and Officers.	NIL
	12/5/18		C.O. attended Conference at Brigade H.Q. at 5 pm. During the morning physical drill was carried out. This was also a Reconnaissance and division of the new line.	NIL
	13/5/18		Physical Training, rifle drill and Box respirator drill. A reconnaissance of new line carried out.	NIL
	14/5/18		During the morning physical training and Harness inspection by C.O. Reconnoitring parties were again sent out.	NIL
	15/5/18		Physical Training and close order drill carried out during morning. Inspection by C.O. A Reconnaissance of new line carries out.	NIL

Army Form C. 2118.

WAR DIARY
INTELLIGENCE SUMMARY.
(Erase heading not required.)

MAY 1918

Place	Date	Hour	Summary of Events and Information	Remarks and references to Appendices
P.20.C.4.5.	16/5/18		Training carried out during morning. Inspection by C.O. Officers reconnoitred new line.	17a
	17/5/18		Physical training carried out during morning. The Battalion bathed. Reconnaissance of new line by Officers. Lt. Col. P.F. HONE M.C. arrived at Battalion H.Q. during the evening.	17a
	18/5/18		3 other ranks surpers to Training Establishment despatches to Base. Reconnaissance of new line carried out Lt. Col. P.F. HONE M.C. assumed Command of Battalion.	17a
O.24.b.5.0.	19/5/18		Sunday. Church Parade. Battalion moved to a more suitable camping ground at O.24.b.5.0. (Sheet 27)	17a
	20/5/18		20 N.C.Os. reconnoitred line with Officers and were instructed in their duties as Guides. Ribbands presented to No. 15060 C.S.M. a. Giles and No. 41013 C.S.M. J. Shelley by the Military General.	17a
	21/5/18	6.30 am	Very hot day. Full marching order inspection by C.O. Bathing Parade.	17a
		9.40	C.O. and Adjutant with late OC 119th T.M.B. reconnoitred new line.	

Army Form C. 2118.

WAR DIARY
–or–
INTELLIGENCE SUMMARY.
(Erase heading not required.)

MAY 1918

Place	Date	Hour	Summary of Events and Information	Remarks and references to Appendices
O.24.f.5.0	22/5/18		Weather, bright and warm. Training was carried on during the morning. Officers proceed on reconnaissance. C.O. reconnoitres SWITCH.	17th
	23/5/18		Fine morning. Physical Training, close order drill and musketry carried out. Officers and N.C.Os reconnoitres HONDEGHEM SWITCH.	17th
	24/5/18		Heavy rain all day. Leaving of new carried out never ever. Roads in bad condition.	14th
	25/5/18		Fine morning. Inspection of Staff by C.O. Inspection of Transport by C.O. Physical training & close order drill carried out. Reconnaissance of new line by Officers.	17th
	26/5/18		Fine morning. G.O.C. called at Batln. H.Q. Captain F. Ashworth & Capt C.E Calvert C.E Calvert reconnoitres new line. Inspection of Camp by C.O.	19th
	27/5/18	10.30 a.m	Fine morning. Officers proceed on reconnaissance of HONDEGHEM SWITCH with N.C.Os. Purposed H.Q. and Company boundaries chosen. O.C. 227th R.I. French army called at Battalion H.Q.	15th

Army Form C. 2118.

WAR DIARY
— OF —
INTELLIGENCE SUMMARY.
(Erase heading not required.)

MAY 1918

Place	Date	Hour	Summary of Events and Information	Remarks and references to Appendices
O.24.4.5.0.	28/5/18		Training in Musketry and Physical Drill carried out.	178
	29/5/18		Fine day. Physical training and Musketry carried out. Officers reconnoitred new line. Awards pub'd. 6S of the Military Cross to Capt. & Adjutant A. G. Symons and the Revd. J. E. M. Watson C.F. (Killed in action 10/4/18).	178
	30/5/18		Morning fine. Physical training carried out. All officers and N.C.Os. reconnoitre new line. Inspection of Camp by C.O.	178
	31/5/18		Fine weather and hot. Officers and C.O. reconnoitres new line. Men bathed at ST. MARIE CAPPEL. Court of Enquiry held re loss of Acquittance Rolls and cash during operations on the 9 April 1918.	178

J. J. Hum.
31/5/18
Lt. Col.
Commanding 21st Bn. Australian Regiment

Army Form C. 2118.

WAR DIARY
or
INTELLIGENCE SUMMARY.
(Erase heading not required.)

21st (S) Bn. Middlesex Regt.

War Diary

June 1918.

Place	Date	Hour	Summary of Events and Information	Remarks and references to Appendices

Instructions regarding War Diaries and Intelligence Summaries are contained in F. S. Regs., Part II. and the Staff Manual respectively. Title pages will be prepared in manuscript.

Army Form C. 2118.

WAR DIARY
INTELLIGENCE SUMMARY.
(Erase heading not required.)

JUNE 1918

Place	Date	Hour	Summary of Events and Information	Remarks and references to Appendices
ST. MARIE CAPELLE	1/6/18	9.30 am / 10.30 am	Hot and fine. Physical Training carried out. Inspection by C.O. During remainder of morning training carried out under supervision of Adjutant.	
	2/6/18	9 am / 10 "	Fine morning. Commanding Officer inspected Camp. Kit inspection. Immediate Award. The award of Bar to D.S.O. to Lt.Col. H.C. METCALFE published.	
WACQUING-HEN	3/6/18		Weather bright and hot. The Battalion proceeded to ARNEKE and entrained. Detrained at MARQUISE and marched to WACQUINGHEN. Battalion went into billets and came under orders of 102nd Infantry Brigade. 34th Division.	
	4/6/18		Fine morning. Billets arranged for 3rd Battn. 309th (American) Infantry Regt. and also Supply Company of same Regiment. The 3rd Battalion were billeted at BEUVREQUEN and the Supply Company in WACQUINGHEN.	
	5/6/18		Fine morning. Capt. J. ASHWORTH and 2nd Lt. J.T. FLORETY attached to 3rd Battn. 309th Infantry Regt. to assist with instruction and training of American troops at BEUVREQUEN.	
	6/6/18		Training of American troops carried out during day in P.T. + B.T. Gas and Musketry. Reconnaissance by C.O. of Training Area. Inspection of Ranges. Lecture by C.O. to Instructors.	
	7/6/18		Training of American troops carried on in Musketry, Lewis Gun, Bayonet fighting, Bombing and Gas.	
	8/6/18		Training of American troops carried on. Construction of Miniature Trench System commenced.	

WAR DIARY
or
INTELLIGENCE SUMMARY.
(Erase heading not required.)

Army Form C. 2118.

JUNE 1918.

Instructions regarding War Diaries and Intelligence Summaries are contained in F. S. Regs., Part II. and the Staff Manual respectively. Title pages will be prepared in manuscript.

Place	Date	Hour	Summary of Events and Information	Remarks and references to Appendices
WACQUING-HEN.	9/6/18		Sunday. Inspection of Billets by C.O. Conference of Officers. Passes granted to some of Training Staff to visit BOULOGNE and WIMEREUX.	
	10/6/18		Training of American troops carried on. Orders received to proceed to LUMBRES AREA where Battalion would come under orders of 101st Infantry Brigade, 34th Division.	
HARDINGHEN	11/6/18		Fine day. Battalion proceeded to HARDINGHEN by march route. End of stage for first day. Transport accompanied Battalion under Capt. F.J. SMITH, D.C.M.	
HAUT LOQUIN	12/6/18		Fine day. Battalion proceeded by march route to HAUT LOQUIN. Arrived in billets 2 p.m. Capt. C.E. CALVERT and Capt F.J. SMITH D.C.M. with 9 other ranks proceeded to TOURNY to be at disposal of O.C. 2nd Bn. 309th (American) Infantry Regt.	
	13/6/18		Lieut. E.M. WELSTEAD and 9 other ranks proceeded to ALQUINES and reported to Lt. Col. Stephenson D.S.O. 16th Royal Scots. Remainder remaining at HAUT LOQUIN to be at disposal of O.C. 3rd Bn. 309th Inf. Regt. Training of American troops proceeded with.	
	14/6/18		Training of American troops carried out.	
	15/6/18		Training of American troops carried out.	
	16/6/18		Sunday. Church parade 9-30 a.m. Some of American troops attended.	
	17/6/18		Training of American troops carried out in Musketry, Lewis Gun, Bayonet Fighting, Bombing and Gas. Regimental School started. Battalion H.Q. removed from HAUT LOQUIN to ALQUINES and Battalion came under orders of 116th Infantry Brigade, 39th Division.	
ALQUINES	18/6/18		Training of American troops carried out. Lieut. T. GRAINGER-STEWART M.C. 16th Royal Scots reported for duty as Musketry Officer.	

Army Form C. 2118.

WAR DIARY
or
INTELLIGENCE SUMMARY.
(Erase heading not required.)

JUNE 1918.

Place	Date	Hour	Summary of Events and Information	Remarks and references to Appendices
ALQUINES	19/6/18		Morning wet but turned out fine later. Training of American troops carried out. C.O. rode up to Training Ground with Col. MORGAN, 309th Infantry Regt.	
	20/6/18		Training of American troops carried out.	
	21/6/18		Training of American troops carried out.	
	22/6/18		1st Bn. 309th (American) Infantry Regt. firing on long range. The Divisional Commander and Staff visited Training Ground with C.O. First Course, Regimental School, closed.	
	23/6/18		Sunday. Church parade 9.15 a.m.	
	24/6/18		Second Course, Regimental School opened, and Lewis Gun School for privates started. Training for American troops carried out. Weather rather wet.	
	25/6/18		Day fine. Training of American troops carried out. Inspection of American troops at training by Second Army Commander.	
	26/6/18		Training of American troops carried out.	
	27/6/18		Training of American troops carried out.	
	28/6/18		Training of American troops carried out.	
BOULOGNE	29/6/18		Weather fine. Orders received for Battalion to proceed to England. Battalion proceeded by march route to Railway Station at NIELLES and entrained for BOULOGNE. On arrival Battalion went under canvas at Rest Camp.	

Army Form C. 2118.

WAR DIARY
or
INTELLIGENCE SUMMARY.

(Erase heading not required.)

JUNE 1918.

Instructions regarding War Diaries and Intelligence Summaries are contained in F. S. Regs., Part II. and the Staff Manual respectively. Title pages will be prepared in manuscript.

Place	Date	Hour	Summary of Events and Information	Remarks and references to Appendices
MYTCHETT ALDERSHOT	30/6/18		Weather fine. Battalion embarked for FOLKESTONE and on arrival entrained for NORTH CAMP STN. ALDERSHOT. On arrival at ALDERSHOT went under canvas at MYTCHETTS and came under the command of the 74th Infantry Brigade, 25th Division.	[illegible]

F. A.
Lt. Col.
Commanding 21st Bn. Middx. Regt.